A Collection of Poetry

Jill Niebuhr

authorHOUSE®

AuthorHouse™
1663 Liberty Drive
Bloomington, IN 47403
www.authorhouse.com
Phone: 1 (800) 839-8640

Published by AuthorHouse 06/16/2016

ISBN: 978-1-5246-1422-5 (sc)
ISBN: 978-1-5246-1421-8 (e)

Library of Congress Control Number: 2016909721

Print information available on the last page.

Dedicated to all the broken hearts

Contents

ON THE EDGE - HAIKU

Who are you?

Credibility
Is armor, might, taste, good sight
Please hold on to me

She's Out of Control

I'm your maniac!
Just another crazy bitch
Yelling at the moon

Power

Fingers on the rock
Shadow pointed, deep edges
For strength to build with

Treatment

Black and hot coffee
Steaming in my Styrofoam
Like an angry boy

Crazy Michael

Crazy Michael stirs
With hundreds of sad stories
Until he will die

Losing my Keys

Going psychotic
Pay the toll and see me pace
Back and forth today

orceo

Smile

Turn those lips around
We don't want to see you frown
Blessing you and me

Numbers

One vulnerable
Adult makes way to freedom
Receiving his number

Schadenfreude

Watching me fall down
Large crowds hasten to make gay
Of my tragedy

Happiness

My grace, mercy, bliss-
Three elements of hope
To hold tightly to

Knowledge

Reading black writing
Conforming my mind to eyes
Where I see clearly

INSIGHT INTO MY ILLNESS AND OTHER THINGS IN LIFE

God

I seek you with intent
Knowing my ways fall short
Instead of the struggle, I find the light.
Instead of thinking, contemplating, and fearing- I trust.
Oh, with you, I believe.
It's amazing to see my dreams come true
In alignment with you
I pray

Tremble

My heart aches
Until the pain resides
Tapping on my fears.

You still tell me not to worry.
It makes me tremble.

I follow blindly.
I want to believe.
I let go.

I allow those words to lead.
Faith runs over my feelings.
Fear is funny.
I am not scared.

It was so easy
To give up.
I feel so much better.
Instead of a tremble
Instead of a tear
I have hope

One day

One day,
All I need
Right now

Now

Don't look back.
Don't jump forward.
You'll lose what's happening
Now.

PTSD

I have nothing to offer
Nothing to say
Everything's fine
I want to keep it that way

What we feed

I've been thinking the same
With the same habits
To feed it.

I could read.
I could listen.

Still I couldn't learn
Until I changed my ways.

I became free
From the thinking I wanted to lose
By changing habits that were burning
A hole in me.

My thinking died down.
My faith grew.
Appreciation set me apart.
And I started to teach others.

Every day
I learn something new.

Honesty is a corner of strength
In me, and others I'm with.

We help each other
As a community.

It's no longer me.
It's us.

I know I'm growing.
I've got old wounds to show you,
To shock you.

If I don't say it,
My smile will evade it.

True Love

♡

Exchanges We Can Appreciate

Untitled

A bird flew by me
So swiftly
Without looking
And how could it fly by
And miss the miracle taking place?

The Mighty

Butterfly, Butterfly,
All Colors in One
Winged as It Come
Flock lighter than some

They call on the butterfly
Stay with me, they pray
Look pretty; while I play
Fly. But Don't Go Away

Don't make a sound
No room on the ground
You think you are free
So flutter me. Please.
Shine all the day
Never Knowing your Way.

Butterfly, Butterfly
There are no words
From the silence of life
A Succulent Herd

The butterfly
Fly by
Me
Flittering and fluttering
So Gracefully

Butterfly, Butterfly
Fly By Me
Again

One day
I'll see
Your Wings stop by

They'll lift me up
So light
Like the weather
When it's hot

As I like it
I prefer you
To grace my presence

In flight
I, too, reign

Fiesty Creator

Creative harmony;
It's what I do best.

When the night falls;
I serenade from my chest.

I keep a closet of lesser virtue-
Big as a mansion.

My, my,
Your shoes are small.
Yes. My indulgences are weak.
I walk away from each
week after week.

Hello.
No one can hear me
Sweep up meat I'll never eat.

Badgered now-
I let you do what you seek.

I contain my own
Without a microphone.

And the pen, full out- bled
My brain coming on strong again.
It makes them weak
What I speak
And Speak
And Speak

La-la-la Lilac

Purple sinks into elegant stems
Past the green stick drawing an ace
Shrubs of syringe lighten my face
Taking over my mind. Erase!

I'm gonna fall
gonna float
Soft and sweet
Like a la-la-la
Lilac.

Heed!
Springing
Straight from the maze
A fragrant gas starts to amend
Pure. It's Pouring, together it bends.

I'm gonna fall
gonna float
Soft and sweet
Like a la-la-la
Lilac.

Timid, I watch to be
Gentle as your tone
Ready for forgiveness
I took you home.

Look at the lilac
Sure doesn't take much
Turn this root around
Run. Now
Catch this glimpse again.

Peach purple majestic stick like a stem
Holding me down the lilac is back again
In this your la-la-la lilac?

I'm gonna fall
gonna float
Soft and sweet
Like a la-la-la
Lilac

A lala lala lilac
Mind like mine erased
Soft and sweet, embrace my taste
Lilac living best and bright.

I'm gonna fall
gonna float
Soft and sweet
Like a la-la-la
Lilac.

Dear, timid, languid, gently
A tone you're stroking in
Forgive my sinful recompenses
I wave so freely
To your gentle step.

I'm gonna fall
gonna float
Soft and sweet
like a la-la-la
Lilac.

As the lilac lifts my head to the trees
Small little fauna of love
Do me to be true
Lilac, goodbye grub
These petals are vibrant
Bringing out my love.

I'm gonna fall
gonna float
Soft and sweet
Like a la-la-la
Lilac.

Living at the Library

I've just got to stop.
I tell myself, Hop!
Don't take too long
You have to get back-
to working on your songs.

There is so much text
I swear; it's better than sex.
Power in every word,
Mysticism; silence can be heard.

Sitting like potato chips,
You can't grab just one.
The subjects are flavors.
Eat them all up!

What's for dessert?
Some fiction
or ones from the back
covered in dirt.

I've got to hurry, but I just can't stop.
I want to keep digging
Around the round clock.

Guiding Light

Guiding light,
Shining bright,
You're all
I got tonight.

A four leaf clover;
Found as I grieve,
Says this is short-lived-
And luck is mine.

My spirit lifts.
I hold on tight,
And bring it home
To store it away.

Guiding light,
Shining bright,
You're all
I got tonight.

An abusive man
Led me to worship the moon.
The star in my eyes
As I made a mix for true love

Conversations with angels
Holding my last breath
The smells, the lights,
The center I held to.

Guiding light,
Shining bright,
You're all
I got tonight.

A wooden dock
Falling apart
Invites me on
To the water's whisk.

Water near it
Glistens
A sea of freshness
Listens.

Guiding light,
Shining bright,
You're all
I got tonight.

Here Is Not There

It is not you.
Mere circumstance,
This situation will pass.
Don't worry!

Stop fussing!
Don't fret.
Save yourself!

Be a gift
In the outward flow,
The graciousness
Of all you are.

As you learn,
You grow.
Give it out.
You'll know.

Don't forget to live.
Life isn't running this.

Parade
Your part.
Don't deny
Your art.

Say I am here
And be there.
No other place better.
No other place right.

Wind moving,
A song comes in.
Nature uplifts.
You are here.

You are here
In our separations.
We are together
In our difficulties.
We will learn
In our strains.
We will be defined
By our strength.

Be as God.
Be as you—
Blessed in your environment,
Steadfast in your hope,
Comfortable in your existence.

Here you are now.
There is no other.
Here is not there.

Here is where you are
You are not coming
Nor are we going.
Where are you right now?

Enjoy me
Enjoying you.
As I said already,
Here is not there.

If it was,
You'd miss the
Whole thing.
Here is not there.

Writing, Writing

Writing, writing,
Write away.
Write the day
Always, always.

Always, always
I'm on the prowl
Of the pen
Tipping again.

Again, again
I need my pen.
This is how
I'm writing, writing.

Writing, writing
Write a way.
Write the day
Always, always.

Hating

Hate
Be me
Hate
Be me
I hate
To be
Me

Give Me More

Baboom da de,
Oh, sweet slayer-
Start beat at it; deep intact
Dee dee da do-
All day long.

Sound sound sound
Love me
Got it on on on
Ground me good.

Give me love
When life is down.
I am yours-
Hound hound hound.

Manipulate ears til I switch
And this keeps on
Round round round.

Move me more
Come on you're
Telling me
Off.

I can't stop
Do it now.
Sweet is how.
Deep
You're dark.
I will.
We will.

We die
To keep you off.

gonna

gonna

C·A·LL

gonna

FLOAT

soft and sweet

like a **Mm**ellalelela

Eladie

Nightfall

Gently it whimper around
Like a creature
a disease
The carrier to the Queen
The city lights
and my life
as a wife

Dedication,
endearment,
my love has me
wearing it

Still
Nothing seen
Not a thing in sight
For never
no part
Close from the start
More white with these lights

Hungry
murders
rape
the call
insomnia

Wait-
for dawn
Shrill victory of night
Fall with my eye
Brain-
hurdle.

Wake.

Night
Fall so slow
Denying the pace
Keep keeping on

Night
Fools
Sight rise in still
No longing
For my limbs to launch
Pieces back
Together I held them tight

Time to sleep never arrives
As fast as it dropped
It whisks ado again

Night fell
then it left.
Once again,
My suffering
Never ends

Aids

Aids,
You want me.
You can't have me.

I'm smarter than you-
Stronger than disease,
I've lived with poison my whole life

You are wrong.
Poisoning our connection;
People spawned to bring it.
You take away.
Aids, go away

Peace must be sublime
You can not have all that you want.
Neither can I.
It is not mine.

Alarm Clock

Sounding loud.
Calling out.
That terrible sound-
That hits you.
You can't
Get away from it.
It will not-
Let me snooze.
It beeps,
Beep!
Beep!

Disrupted

Rain,
Fall a little harder if you can cleanse my tainted soul.
Wash away weariness. Show me how to follow bliss.
Play along where you belong.
It's there you'll find your precious kiss.

Thunder,
Crack as hard as you may.
Leave me-
Without a thing to say.
Snatch a limb onto the ground. Make it shake for your sound.
A point is true you've surely made.
Make silence rumble,
Turn black to jade.

Snow, fall soon.
Cover the earth to hide the dirt so I can see your worth.
Shower the treetops as you cover the land.
You're high and mighty,
No need for a hand.

Sun, shine a little brighter.
You light up the world.
Blind blue to become carefree.
As a day is done you tuck away
Just to shine onto a brighter day.

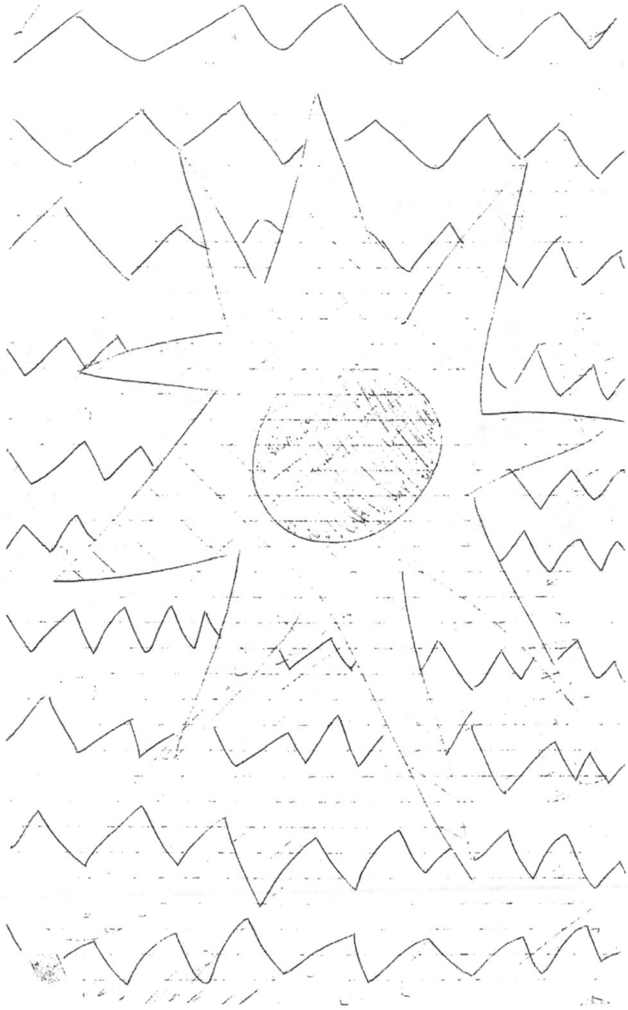

Nowhere

Nowhere,
No. Where?
Do you know where that's at?

Man said, "No. Where?"
Said, I don't know either,
But I sure got there fast.

Tell me a tale of escape:
A bridge, maybe to somewhere
If I don't want to be there.
It must be better than nowhere.

Pardon me, walk lost its roll.
Somewhere it fell.
I have nothing to hold.
I'm crying love rotting dead,
Soaking in misery,

Die. I am dying
A pathetic death.

Boy

Boy,
Stand up.
Stay out of them streets.

Man in your hand,
You're a woman with heat.

You can't?
Sorry, neither could I.
You will lie.
You will see.
Someone will die.

With your eye,
Probably be
Where you die too-
On the corner
With the steps.

Hitting,
I've met
It all
In my sight.
On the street,
In the night,

Get out if you can, boy.
I don't want you to die.
I don't want you to cry.

This is not a lie.
People in the streets lie,
But the streets don't.

This could be your end.
Mine may be here, too.
Just thought I'd reach out to you.

It's life or death in these streets,
And the life ain't worth living,
The death a small sacrifice.
A memorial will be placed
If you don't get out alive

People will forget.
Hell, they won't know
All your potential.

Start living anew.
Pull your pants up!
Get away from them drugs.
Give'em up!

Life isn't here, so
Get out while you can.
Don't be another mystery.

Figure it out.

To Believe Is Naïve

Across the dust bench, o'er the puddled bridge,
Under a door of cobwebs you must cross.
Hold tight. There's no choice.
Alas! A
Blow of clear air with no prize
What could I expect? What could I say?
To Believe
Is Naïve.

In Light

In light
I dance as the lasers' toll
Swing around like a swimmer's throw
Till I sleep a sleigh that rides mourning away
Tasting like ice seeping further the brain
I follow the feeling. I follow the heat
The light

In light
A Stretch so deep is sown
A unifying color blind my eyes
The Horizon circumcised
Rest in the feeling, I rest in the heat
The light

In light
The brightness will not take no
The silence will not consolidate
Does not enjoy to cooperate

Darkness can't find
What these rays decide
A voice defines my vein inside
I lie in the feeling. I lie in the heat
The light

Screen Saver

Computer aided chip- snipping away.
Megabytes of memory. Voodoo's insane.
Too many mad nights
J-A-M-M-E-D
Into a head ahead, that's filed tight.
Frightening foes,
Scary sounds,
Single hormones,
Formed like clowns.

Giggling gigabytes-
Laughing hyenas.
Everything's so funny
Once I've cleaned up.

An internet of amusement-
5 rows of paradise,
Click clock. Click clicking,
Till everything stands as vice.

Space

Space – ah,
Yes.
Space. Ah,
Separate that. Not
U are not
Separating me.

Out of Minnesota

A state seems so small.
My heart is not-
Cannot crawl
When it traps in the mind
Nothing to find.

You're given your mind-
Nothing to search.
Individual, I find
Gets huddled in the middle.

All the tears trail into lakes
Until there's 10,000 some
Polluted in place.
Lade, slip her a slipper.
She'll be fine in the morn'.

They know best,
So my dreams are laid to rest.

It's not best-
My free land put to the test

Was it the lakes that took her captive?
Was it the cold that cracked my love?
I swear the wind blew us in.
They couldn't get out.

Marry Minnesota? Never-
Never will I
Allow my personal prayer
To remain under my hair.

Hear here,
I shout my prayer out
To keep me safe from the state,
So it never search me out.

The state that made my safety sound
Is now a place to hide around.
I feel betrayal.
It's all around.
This state has me searching
For a fun place-
One of joy.

My misery abound.
It leaps around.
It calls you out.
Trouble so near.
Let me out.

The Power

I light up
To escape.
Makes me feel powerful
To drop my mind.
Pick up the pipe.
Light it all away.

I run to it.
I jump on it.
I prance.
Ovulate.
I laugh at the others
Who are straight.

Spawning my soul
'Til I am enclosed
In delicate worlds
Where I am scattered
In pieces,
I feel whole.

The moon blinds me.
I creep like a vampire
To my next victim,
My next inmate.
This brightens my life-
My guide in strife.

Tunes thicken.
They make no sense.
I thought I got it.
I thought wrong.

Here I am;
Jubilous one.
Sustain me.
Crackling with Glee,
Be gone, tears.
My fears I forget.
This is how
I live.

I prance. Ovulate.
I hate those tears
Causing my fears
To escape
To this state.

This power is not mine.
I hold it dearly.
I know no other.
Come on,
Get near me.

In Front of Me

Fountain
Flows
My brain awes
Far away, far from small.
If I were a fish I wouldn't dream to walk.
If I couldn't drink I couldn't talk.
I let it flow. It goes away.
War of the future held today.
More people?
Then we need more water.
Global warming will not holler.
We fight for oil our bodies don't want.
We fight, of course, so that we can flaunt.
Being so needed that it's raped
Brings about this terrible fate.
Water in front of me
Far away
War of the future
Abused today

Used to grow food
Take blood head to knee
Keeping my skin
Thick and clean.
It's pumping my heart
Sensing my veins

Water in front of me
Is far away
War of the future
Abused today

Watch Me Fail

I am water.

Watch me fall.
Watch me float.
Watch me fly.

I am water people need.
Here for a purpose.
Here, and I hate it.

I am abused.
I am weak.
I am sore.
Clear as can be.

Disregard.
Overlooked.
Treated-
Like a crook.

Accessory,
Look naught.
Because I am clear.
Silent in thought.

Wonders of the World.
Wonderful me.
Cherish I ask.
I have no greed.

Give them Fear
What's in this lake?
Give them Fear.
Show how they hate.

Watch me flow.
Watch me go.
Then watch them break.

The Water Fall
Will Fail.

PRESIDENT

P erson
R ewarded by
E nduring
S uffering
I n order to
D evelop an
E ntity
N ecessary for
T ruth

Music In The Air

I.
Hear me in the air
Watch me if you dare
I'll dance in your speaker
I'll return but not weaker

II.
Let me listen to your story
On how you made it through
Each night I came through.
Listen. I'll tell you.

III.
Let me lift you up.
I'm in the air.
You can hear me. Touch me.
Tell me it'll be alright
For I came through tonight.

IV.
Tell me how you're mine.
You know I am the kind
that will see you through.
I'm the kind that is true.

V.
The rare value of my price
Will come through
Every time I'm up
So turn me up.

VI.
Fill me up with the volume
I embrace
the kind you cannot chase
the kind you will enjoy

My Pen

My Pen is My Sword.
The fighting batillion.
Feel my hardship.
Sharp around the edges.

COMMAND CENTER

Freedom

Freedom is not a dream.
Freedom is a desire.
Freedom is a destiny.
Freedom is being.
One cannot be
Without freedom.
So, don't lose who you are.
Hold onto your freedom.

Living on the Edge

Living on the edge,
I never thought to look down.
Only straight ahead.
A telescope of forced beliefs and tainted accusations.
I lingered on the tip.
Never looking down.

Then I did.
I looked down.
Then I jumped.
A sea of euphoria
Came around.

My own fantasies and dreams.
A capsule of my wildest wishes.
A capsule with two open ends
And no circumference.

Now.
There is no edge.
There is a sea wide as the sky.
There is no telescope.
There is me.

The devil I tantalized with is the bulk of my last nightmare.
I killed the devil guilty of an eighteen year torture.
I won.
I became one.

To Be Young and Free

Looking at the city lights.
Full aware
Anger's got the best of me tonight.

Starting now
As innocent as a baby's breath

Then I step out to where those lights are
Never knowing what I'm in for.

I feel young and free!

All that white, glaring my eyesight.
Only few colors sustain on clear nights

Some towered up so high-
Like my ego.

It takes a plane
To fly by alright.

Inspiration IS Everything

ARE EVERYTHING——————
IS ALL——————
IS IT——————
WITH THIS——————
IS NOTHING——————
AINT SHIT——————

Old Ways

I'm where the cold lays
Where the frost is bitter.
I sleep in old ways.
Time is a critter.
No litter do I lay
No waste in my game
My life is wicked
Where the cold lays.

The Pleasure Principle

I'm going to
Wipe off the hurt.
Choose to take pleasure.
Make life much better
Befriending the pleasure.

Victory

Vision 2
Ignite
Cornerstones
Toward
Outcomes
Retarding
Yesterdays

Daredevil

Beware.
This life's toxic.

I go in and out,
Up and down,

Oh my God-
All around.

I fall.
I get up.

I lose my way.

I find
I can
Continue
Like this.

Unforbidden

Free.
So free.
Let me make mistakes.
I'm becoming me.
What a way to go.
How I know
This way
Is the only way I know.

Confusion

It echoes in my ear. Sounds
As I tear at my hair.
Pulling slowly,
So it hurts.
My muscles tighten
And I feel better
For a brief second.

My psychotic eyes daze
At nothing.
I feel the hurt
But it tingles.
Should I cry? Fight? Scream?

My body tightens.
I want to shake it out.
Go away.
My head keeps beating to the music

It is still there.
Echo in my ear
The sounds I heard
Continuing to hear
I pull so slowly
So it hurts
So my muscle expands
And for a second, peace continues.

Psychotic gaze
When the eyes see nothing
As I hurt for nothing
Tingling for a move
I frustrate my indecision – sigh-

If I could shake it out
If I could
If the thought can bake
My head
Confusions still there, frustrating I wait
For my thought of clean air

Fire of My Fury

No God am I- mortal, shallow, and angry
The Fire of My Fury is a temple
Unscathed by compassion.
I walk amidst the other sinners
Not to add joy to their days,
But to strike down
Challengers who
Step up to me to play.
Have you watched it?
Have you noticed my smile has completely faded away?
I am arisen by its call.
Worn out I fall down
And I dream of the time when
The ball scatters from my mind,
The time something greater will lift me up,
The moment it will no longer be me,
Myself with such a burden to begrudge.
The Fire has come to worn you all-
But I'm so cold, I can't feel it at all.

I can pretend to love myself

I can pretend I love myself.
I don't need you.
I'm on my best.
I can pretend I share great things.
With others, I am gold.
With you, I am rust.

I'll pretend to love myself
When they're so cold.
They could be sculptured.
I'd rather be alone.

I'll pretend I love myself.
I can be left on the stage.
Whimpering, whining,
It's all a game.

I'll be taking a right of left.
I'm not straight with you.
It's straight off the cliff.
I scat. I say.
I fascinate the soft.
I can pretend
I love myself.

When I pretend
I love myself
I no longer need you.

Stuck

I am stuck.
A pattern-dyed blanket.
Swish to the Nike.
Hair engaged.
Remote child.
A dog raising his paw.
Like dirt, stuck to the ground.

I am stuck.
No right
To my wrong.
Leaving what rests.
No spring to life.
No closing the door.

It's open.
I'm stuck.
Loving your fame
When I'm
Hating my name.
Loving you.
Hating me.
It's all stuck.
I'm going nowhere.
Can't you see?

Appeal to the rhythm

Your heart would think it sweet
To know you know it all
Revolves around a beat

Two

I am worn
By two feet that
Waddle when
Asked a question.
Two arms
Protecting me
From big men.
Two eyes
Rolling all the way
Around.
Two ways to do things
Right or wrong

Death Becomes Her

Midnight chimes at the
Psychiatric outlaw
While pain echoes
From freedom's restraint.

Death becomes her.
Wholly, fully,
Encapsulating hope,
Stealing joy,
Masking glory
To a despondent state.

Death Becomes her.
Watch out!
Her mind is alive.
It's on the run again.
I need to run again,
Yet all I got it doors,
One room,
A hall,
A portion of a floor.

Death becomes her.
Too late to live.
Too gone to give.
Too bright to give in.
It feels like death
Living like this.

The Witch

A liar gave the girl life.
A violent, alcoholic gave her bruises at night.

Odds and ends comprised her life
She could not discern this
Not which is which.

The girl was lynched, hitched and snitched on
Her stitches were barriers
But she chose to live on.

At night,
She escaped the memories
In different ways.

On a full moon
She found her best
Was left by the firelight.

Guilty

Guilt invades my will.
I stall.
I feel it cringing inside,
Invading my mind,
Helplessly imposing
A burden on my worth.

Guilt travels
Across the ribs
Down my body, my
Chest hollow
Elbow, my shoulders,
All crunched up.

You can see with your eyes.
Not needing to move, you can see it all in
My physical form.
Where is my worth?

Trail of Years

Are you mad, Jill?
Have you fallen?
Have you stumbled?
Can you not pull through?

I want this for you:
Good things-
Peace,
Balance,
And love,

Oh, Love,
Give it up.
Grant her sweetness.
Put it in your pocket.
Tend to its care.

Harmony,
In love and from above.
I want you to see things better.
I want to walk with you.

I will be your friend, Jill.
Just come with me
On this journey
As no other has walked before.

Hunger and Thirst

Near to me in here.
New vacancy from filled.
Severing down a slope severe.
Of craving lack the coping crane.

Starvation in the street, single-
We would make the perfect pair.
Should we? To meet.

Open up. Come inside. Let's go take a ride.
My tummy's talking. Throat's torn.
The eye can't see a hurt stain.
Sneaking off- we need to dance
In the rain
On our feet.

When we meet
You will find
You've been hungry all this time.

"Agua, Senor"
I feel fried at the scene
Quit teasin, trippy ticky phene
I'm dyin' right here.
Come back through that door.

I Am A Woman

I am a woman. It's been a long time.
They say that a man will show me what's mine.
I haven't found the family they talk of.
I pave the way for life to be full of
Power and wealth, that isn't the norm
Women walk around completely torn.

I am a woman masked by their ideas.
Children grow quick and change how they see us.
I'm building today on yesterday's lessons.
No man helps me. That thought I rest on.
There comes a time when the past is gone.
As a woman, I hope to live long.

I am a woman. I am not without value.
I claim the best. Ask me. I'll tell you.
There is not a man who will hold me down.
Raise me high or be without a sound.
My destiny I make. My fate is on a test.
I am woman – unlike all the rest.

I Am Heart

Let me be.
I am alive.
Working on my own.
Gathering life from my support.
Pumping juices everyday.
I am heart.

Let me beat.
I am static
Too close you cling.
So step back.
And let me work.
I am heart.

Let me bleed.
I am new everyday
I let the old wash away
You're no longer needed for my sustenance.
Quit trying. You're gone.
I am heart.

Let me Flee.
I fly so high.
You'd swear I was an eagle.
I stay so long.
You'd swear I was a condor.
Waiting you off.

Pumping around.
I am heart.

Let me be free.
I work unrestricted.
I live less conflicted.
I am on my first legs.
Pumping juices everyday.
I am heart.

Let me be.
Let me beat.
Give me blood.
I am heart.

Let me flee.
Let me be free.
Let me breathe.
I am heart.

Half and half

Racing. Roaring. Ravishing.
Still
I sit.

Leaping. Leering. Longing.

Quiet-
I remain.

Embodied. Exhilarated. Emergent.
Questioning,
I think.

Doubt lock me up.
Spirit, set me free.
This soul burns
In a river of oils.

Scentist's thrill.
My heart is half hero
And half coward.

Still
I sit.

Darkness

Darkness escapades again.
Taking me back to a night.
I haven't yet fought for.
Never-ending.
Silent calls.
Remote thoughts flash.
My thinking won't stop.
I am still.
Moving cops.

Nothing to be seen.
Not a thing in sight.
That's what you'd think
If you didn't see a light.

Murders still happen.
Rapes go on.
Hunger still lingers.
Kids wait for dawn.
Arsonists light.
They think they're so cool.
Prisons are packed
Why were they such fools?

Senseless Sleep

My eyes closed.
My brain awake.

Longing for my limbs to launch
To a sleeping abyss.

Frozen fragments
Of a worn out gal.

What is left of this date?
Who is calling to me?

It is no use.

I close my eyes to
Flashes of insanity.

When I open my lids,
A welcoming light
Whispers through the palm tree.
White.

It is senseless.

Alertness shocks
A tired body, aching forehead.

I am controlled
By a living mind.

Let me sleep and sleep.
No.
My ligaments kick, turn, and curl.

It is not time yet.
Where is that light switch?

Despondency of Miracles

Watch on

Full flesh
> Gushing from the brain

Tackled scars
> Lie in vain

Hearts made of stone
> Crimes untold

Knees scraped
> Ankles bruised

Arms broken
> Guns and voodoo

Shots fired
> Dreams escaped

Emptiness and death is all that remains

Addicts are poison.
Filled with lies.
Armed with a smile
When they step out.

Meet the day.
The one you can't see.
Look at all
That's destroyed your reality.

Addicts cry.
Poor me. Boo hoo.
I'm just a sucker
For being one, too.

What's Always Hot

Do you like the sound of fire?
The bass of thunder?
The birds say,
"Oh yes, oh, yes, I am
Singing- I can. I sing. I can."

What I'm doing right now:
Trying to come up with a piano rock tune.
Newest conception:
Beaded flyers.
First time: having surround sound!

What's the best best dance movie?
Are your moves hotter?
Who should be president?
Where is the next big thing?

Catch it!
The next trend
May be behind you
Again.

The Artist's Journey

Poetry by my side,
Music of my life,
Melody by and by.

Free Life,
Day to day,
Bird in sky.

Open my mouth.
Embrace my life.

Strength begins
At the end,
Subtle and true,
Be who you knew.

Feels Good to Cry

So long it took to find,
I'm not afraid to cry.
I'd rather fall and die
Than hold it all inside.
Lost, I cannot find
The way to turn
Without tears that burn.

Gone

I am ready to let go
Like a mother whose seen her children grow,
A father who's done his work,
An older sister who's exhausted.

I'm loosening my grip,
Becoming at ease,
I have accepted this is the way it will be.
I have come to terms with my wrong.
I've done my work.
I'm gone.

Sober Woman

Yawheh,
Womanhood.
Sacred entrance to love & hope.

I come to you
Honest and true.

In your likeness
I was made.

I'm grand.
I fall to my knees.

To find part of me
I lost along the way.

I found it too.
I am anew.

True Intent

Goodbye, Pain. Adios, Misery.
I'm leaving to prance on, worth of my life.
Moving on from here.
There's no turning back.

I'm going to meet the gems and precious jewels of life. I'm
going to play
With the other princesses and embrace my strapping prince.
The time is right, the moment clear.

Shall I turn to greet the devil again, I will blast his skanky soul
by choosing blindness.
I only wish to turn and walk away
Proudly.
Proud of being me, a power I have and will use.

I am to flourish in my solitude once again.
I will captivate the status calling,
Strengthen the chains.

The power is used with the same respect I have for it
In a restless soul with so much trueness.
To be noble. I am inside myself & free.
So noble. So real.
That's what life is all about
To me.

Die Away

Sometimes I can not help but wonder if the world just wishes for me to die away.

Am I to fall to the ground like a leaf on an autumn day?

Am I to seep 10 feet under like the raindrops of May?

Should I melt into a puddle after my beauty fades?

Shall I burn your skin red only to leave without a trace?

Tell me, O' Wise One,
Is my stain here to stay-
Or have I just dropped to slowly die away?

Amen

Amen Amen
that I'm fresh as the sea
salty as the ocean
deep as one life
can be horrid, sweet
like a wild animal
hungry for meat
thirsty despite my languid roll
dying though I've never lived completely
loving too much
for always longing
for a touch
so wide you can't see
so real you'll be blinded
completely

When Death is a Blessing

When death is a blessing
The days don disappear.

Graves are the ringing
I hear in my ears.

When death is a blessing
I have lost all hope.

I want the connection
Who brought it so.

Death.
That's what I want.

Death would be a blessing.
My arms could unfold.

With death I turn grave.
I'm sore from hexing.

Death would be a blessing.
Days' dawn.
Nigh disappear.

Graves ringing
As I'm singing
Deep in my ears.

The ZZZs

ZZZ's ZZZ's
Where I start.
Pick up pieces.
They fell apart.
When you can't see catch.
When you can't be you bet.

I dart to the pillow.
Down to head.
Count up to ten.
Go again.

Black ness, clear my mind.
Until with the devil I wine and dine.
Knight in thy bed.
Whispering my head.
All that's meant.
What's meant to be said.

I.d.

I.
I am not me.
For me is not to be found.

I.
I no longer exist
For me is covered in a deceitful world.

Buried.
I am not found.
Amidst anxiety.

I am captured by evil.
I am torn with lies.
I am not me.

Haven't been for awhile.
It's so confusing.
To be and not to be.

Me.
I am.

Envious Seas of Emotion

I'm not to be obliged by a gift that denies.
I won't be aside. Grounds shake inside.
I couldn't allow sorrow for these eyes
Though they cannot cry.
Sound out a lie but not that gift.
I have covered my hills in it.
It's rested between my thighs.
I have seen that mountaintop.
My greediness lies. My servitude I hide
When the shores of the sea
Leave my hands empty
Who takes and who turns that
Sea into envy. Much obliged.

I have to hide

I have to hide switching brain to black.
I can't think this great black will stay empty.
I won't answer it's ringing.
It's too loud to be singing.

I have to hide when I go out.
Scrunch low and won't talk.
I hang out in foreign places.
No one can know me.

I am the scenery's shadow,
A fish lapping a bowl.
I make myself
To not react.
I cannot be reached
For I will not.
No reason, excuse,
Nothing much at all.

Attendance

Happy for Spring
Happy to spring
To attention
And have intent

I ain't the President

I ain't the President.
No Congressman you'll find
Searching through my storage,
Breaking up my mind.

I ain't the President.
No Father am I.
He is doing good things.
I am doing mine.

I ain't the President.
He just hits rewind.
Searching through my storage,
Breaking up my mind.

It's Too Late To Care

It's too late to care.
Too late to fly.
Too far from feeling.
Too far from the sky.

Never a dull moment-
Why ain't it sharp?
Why ain't it clear?
I'm left in the dark.

I'm left in the cold
Without a spark.
It's too late to care.
My prayers have gone dark.

Just Another Broken Promise

Just another broken promise.
Just another beat up dream.
Sighing so soft, you'd think I'd leave.
To go where my amends are stored.
Another promise, hoping for more.

Just another broken Promise
While I'm trying to leave
To wander far away from home.
Another promise as I go.

Just another broken promise
Another day is gone. Another way is clear.
More words I don't need to hear.
My heart's estranged from my dear.

IN MEMORIUM

American-made

I'm God's child.
Set apart from the rest.
Breathing life wherever I go.
Shining like a star.
Living like there's no tomorrow.
Today is all I need.

So far I've come
Being American-made.
I can reach the ends of the Earth.
I overcame disaster karma-free.
I love others and I'm loving me.
When you feel sad I'll take you by the hand.
Never leading to trouble.
This country is my double.

Show Me the Way

Show me the way.
Guide me through the rain.
Surrender mistake
Made on the way.

Show me the way.
I don't have a place.
All meaning is lost.
All continues.
Erase.

Whatever's been done
Can never
Be won.
I really want
To see the truth.
What's going on with me
In the one life I have?
I can't be thrown from the land.

Who needs
Who?
Besides
I need you.
With no understanding
I only feel blue.

A Granddaughter's Love

Low as the moon to pierce like the coon
Wheat thins crunch at the people's brunch
To keep in the mind my favorite hunter
That helped me get all my pets
Gentle but ill
Still so still
My grandfather's death will have to do
If he asks about love, tell him I still do

Secrets

Deeper down than the pits of hell
Flows my fountain of wisdom
Of hope to rise again,
Of faith in my own everlasting.

Faith has intrigued me to peak
And lying down brings me to greater state,
Of time erased, I replace
Burdens built from the wrongs of time,
Well-intentions sprouted weeds
That a moment embraces and aligns.

My hopes cannot be for what was or what is
A woman can hold not only the world
But the devil dressed in full trim
Slim to think what I saw, to be complete
Is never all, for when I fall
I take a flow to all that's great.
You'll never know.

I didn't shout

My brain unwinds so no thoughts are mine
Birds in the distance rays of sun nearby
My head holds it all like a wave with the water
Lapping and tapping at the crisp air
Nothing of people so I don't belong
I cheat and seat myself sneak a peak
This is not life oh I wish
To bury my body in an amazon of green
Colors vivid blending some timid
I like to walk upon the chaos with control
My mind is a cloud when it rains
Like a lion I have a big mane
Insane they say but I call it cool
I call it mine. So reality stood
Small and they thought it so big
This silence it rings
Stays so stout
With a knock at my door
I do not come out
The pain does not hurt
It just drips out and away
I didn't shout

Pride

Smiling, he saw through her eyes.
Fear kept her at bay.
She had to make her own way.
She had so little to say.
He wondered on.
Oblivious
To what was lost.

Belonging

Family is becoming.
It is of value.
Family matters.
It is as I gather.

Parents, sisters, brothers
At the top of the food chain,
At the top of my mind,
The first I call
When I've lost my mind.

We should adhere to the twist
Which can develop with time,
It is ok.
Family understands.
Family minds.

We grow together
With work,
Together with reciprocity,
Together as one.

We move
To build our arks
And share time.
Talk of good ol' days
Is talk of family time.

Together we work.
Together we build.
We become
Family
Over time
For one,
For all,
For unity.
Family time.

Not the Fight

A Petrarchan sonnet

One guard, Sergio, waves thru bodies of blood
Pouring to the puddles feeling the crook
Buzzards above tell the sun, breakfast, lunch, potted on the mud
Sergio in search of which is Bud
Asleep with armor, Bud won't be back to Brook.
Bud's face says no sadness had the time to look
Sergio sneaks to the pond to drain his thumbs with suds
Never did he fear a death he brought near
And now here's the warrior that sheds not a tear
All is tucked in to a distorted sight
Over where it began all the way to right here
The feeling is dead along with his friends, dear
To the heart was the win not the fight.

September 30, 2006

I don't know why I love him so much. The thing is I do. This is the undying, put all my flowers in one basket, unabashedly bold and shameless following of two hearts that somehow came together. Our souls are a beautiful combination. Somehow we only have followed that scary sight a bit. It's too much for us to handle. We try. We tried. Still the times fell short, they fall such many times many nights. I do not regret this feeling. I do not care if he shall turn on me again. I am a person who never came out. Now I refuse to stay in. Jill Niebuhr must be on the plate.

He has given me more value for life than anyone ever before. He found the way to unlock my gates and let the girl who the woman struggles to accept but forever. There's no turning back. There are no regrets.

Light it up.

T.A.

Teasing Ache
One moment
Or more. It was natural to go thru weekends
With a pal who could be honest
When it was no longer a charm.

A Big Brother,
He said. Suspicions caught in my head.
All I ever weakened for
Found God but no one to confide it with

So out of nowhere
As movie plots go, my desire was captured
Though I didn't jump for joy
I was there for every word
But I must keep the state
That invited such a glorified gift and guide

Say I had jumped
Screeched that he was just
All I ever wanted
Would it have alarmed him
Before I take a breath in
I would blink
Find him home again

Or would it, say, make him
Too excited, I will say,
And you know that I mean
Then I would not have got a Big Brother
It could have caused him to exploit

But las, oh, let's just say
A little bit igniting thy soul to this uncertain world
Would have made his day.
I would still be his little girl
And he could a stayed around

I hurt so bad I couldn't
Halt getting it out
And it never docs stop

It plays with my time.
Disappearing all the time,
Then getting me right when it should
Right where I could have changed eternity,
If I was that powerful
And bring him back to me

In a spiteful, derogatory world
Spoiled with destruction, one
Overwhelmed with new life
A stranger took to my side
From a crowd one night
The same crowd I go seeking
The one always get
And he did what I tried
By looking in the bottles at the end of one I'd find

Peace of mind beyond what I can offer
Only to others could I grant something so proper
Oh, I thought
It comes to you
Thank God he did, too
For an arm around my neck
Was about all I required,
Kind words & forgiveness when I
Acted without considering another's effect from it

I wanted so little. He gave so much
If I could step back, I still wouldn't know how to
Show I truly appreciated the comfort he gave
Without acting silly or smearing our bodies
In new discomfort skin

Don't Take My Boy

Time.
Took me.
Told him no one was present.
When I lost him
He held it in his palm.

Time.
Take me.
Come back to my arms.
The grace of you near.

So silly. No fear.
See it for what it is.
All it has lacked.
Hold your ground.
On your knees
Or your way back.

She made me feel special

A woman's so precious.
This woman-
Extreme. Reason I rave for
My heart will complain
That she built virtues
From her heart she made.
Precious as fur, from the animals they're stealing
She made me feel special, her presence's healing.

A head at work and fear at home,
Conversation is spice to make me feel special
Like the wind and the anger and never would she hold.
The gold she is say,
Her heart still heart
On the worst of days,
Her heart is my heart
On the best of days,
But her heart was strong-
Paying years for a day.

I didn't fall from her womb
But she's my mom,
Best friend too. Other ears choose to cruise
And I see her listening. Words will never do.

This heart
Was mine-cause she gave it to me.
Those who wanted it
Got it.
She was a Saint to me.
This saint inside she designed to come out.
All that she gave me is all I will save
For
No longer are these memories here and there
They are with me now, with me, everywhere.
I get to keep her.
The pain of loss has paid.
Her soul is in mine
And it pervades.
Worth preserving,
Worth embracing,
I never could let go.
Time still passes away,
And no matter how high I rise
I'll still be looking up
For what she gave me.
She never passes-
Not for a single day.

Words Hurt

Obscenities of hate splash against the lips.
She snaps her eyes to meet the pink contrast
Blood shot eyes
She walks afraid to stop
Head focused on the cracked pavement
And the words

She only wanted to be loved.
Nurtured. Cared for.
The way she cared.
Her love is not monogamous.
A love so great cannot be focused.
Yearning to exhibit love
She has never felt.

No one can understand
Why?
Good feelings have only brought hate
Now,
Instead of love,
She gets words.

Coming Clean

A long expired telegram
You thought I sought more money
I have been so wrong
I have been so bad
How could I have put you through all that I had
Mad. Glad. Sad. Had I never been neutral?
The world turns away
And the family steps in
An important lesson I needed to win
Today, tomorrow seems much better
But I cannot loosen that grip
For in that sad circumstance
I will put the ones who mean the most to me
Through some more fits.
So many I could write
So many I could thank
But this one covers all of them
And it is sent with Rick's black ink.

I want to warn
The days are hard
I want to tell
I feel on guard
Scared I'll sleep
It will all be worthless
I know you wouldn't say so
Not your guess

I don't want this to be sad
But all the Prozac in the world won't take it away
As successful stunning electric elegant
I may be outside
Inside
There is s terrible war
Harder
Harder
Harder
To fight off.

I dream that love can take it away
My problem then
Is I know not how to love.
I can't love myself
But I love what I do
I can't hold that drink off
Cause it's doing exactly what I want it to
I feel strongly this was
I feel strongly like that
What I feel the most
Is that the hurt will be the end
And it haunts me like a ghost
Everyday

I know it is a matter of time
Holding it off
Makes no sense to me
But here I am
Nothing less.

I am not the bright light
This paper is.
My world is what I make
And writing is what I have to give
It hurts me when others love me
Because I am really not it
I cannot give people
The right kind of encouragement.
The love flowers music
Whisk my days
But when I am not tuning
I fall all these ways.

My fate is death
That makes us the same
But mine will come sooner
If only this were a game
Tears like rain
Smiles for gay
Another day
In time you will blame

You should hate me for me
I do it's true
I hate how I am
And that nothing can change
It no matter what I do
I hate I can't be more
I hate I am no less
I never thought
So much hate
Could be bundled in such a mess

I love you
I love you
And it's here to hurt bad
Another sad story
A linger with no glory

Call Him Kind

She breaks a nail and starts to wail.
He gets the letter grade "B" and goes to drink away the hurt
that bleeds.
Times get tough and people are forced to get rough.

Someone dies and all I can do is sit like louse
Wondering why

Marriage bound break
Every night Mom drinks until she hacks up
No more, push 'n' slides from dad
Don't cry mama, he is only mad

I tried to let you in
When he locked you out because he was afraid that you sinned
I tried to help but then I got smacked
I was no help, good like you
For the whack

And you,
When you lose your temper
Attacking dad with the cookie cutters
I didn't think you had it in you
But I found those court papers in your room

The ones that said dad didn't want me when you two were through
He doesn't like it when I stand up to him
He says I wore him out thin
And I catch him all the time
When he's snooping and hitting

My friends call him "kind."

This matrimony is meant to melt
Mom takin the bottle
Dad making the war
Don't cry when he steams and storms

I tried to let you in
When he locked you out
I got smacked
I was no help, good like you
For the whack

He treats me so young
Even if I am the kid

He doesn't like
When I stand up to him
He says I wore him out thin
I catch him every time
When he's snooping & hitting

My friends call him "kind"

Not My Fault

I've gotta move on
Past drama
You've been giving me

I feel your pain
Every time you leaving me
You go to her

We couldn't last
No matter how I try.
It's not my fault
I'm not the one who lied
It was her

She calls you names
Tells you off like a game
She breaks promises
Cries in your arms.
I shouldn't know all this
I'd be better off

She doesn't like you
Trust you or care
Yet when it comes down to it
You choose her
You're quite a pair

Why you telling me all this?
You know my feelings' strong.
You probably can see it
It's all her.
It's not my fault.

Seeds to Swallow

The pain is so livid
From a knife the eye clears
My upset needs reception
And I sit in rejection
So hectic how short
How I appreciate-still need
Truth & telling & a little less yelling
What more you want from me
Less talk more stop forgetting I mend my bleeds
I sow the seeds that grow tomorrow
I will dread
If I don't see what I have
Before
I
Swallow

Toes

She thinks lying is okay
Then she gets her way
Just tell 'em you're sick
When you're not
I'll tell you I lost it
So I can keep it
I'll tell you, you need to drive
Then change my mind

She teaches others
How to live without boundaries
How to be needy
How to step on people's toes

Then she prays
For other things she wants
Because it's all about her

Easy lies

I wish you would lie to me
Tell me that everything will be okay
I'm so lonely
No one's here to hold me

Tell me my life is not a crying shame
I can see the truth
If you say it
I can play it
Make it go away

Tell me to trust my enemies' strong breath.
Trust me.
It's easier that way
Tell me to tremble in fear
When that don't work
I've seen what I can do
There's cause for nightmares

Tell me my life is not meant to be lived.
So I can give in again
And again
If I never give up
I won't go down again

Tell me beauty sweetens a glare
I've seen you stare
I'm used to life like this

Don't you dare
Tell me my world isn't a fantasy
You don't know how I'm living
Tell me my voice don't need to sing

Tell me a laugh is contagious
Cause I've heard you laughing
And I can't feel a thing

Tell me in all I've lost
I still have depth

I don't think this is it
But you tell me it is
And then act like it's okay

Sweet lies,
I have none to give

My life is meant to be lived
But it'd be easier if it wasn't

I want to give up
I'm so scared
And lonely

You tell me nothing at all
Another lie
I can tell

Stone Season

Lightening strikes my brain
Dead bodies across my floor
Thunder,
It echoes in my heart.
I am stoned cold.
Immaculate only by the eye.
Sensitive only to the true.
And the weak falls into my veins.

Like rain seeping for the ground
I seep for mi amor
The death
Like my friends'

A questioning concentrate draws me near
A VOLATILE CRASH HAS ME HOOKED

I CAN NOT LEAVE
BUT I AM LOST

My body I do not own
It is another
And I am a froth of darkness
Captured by concern

O Venus

Evicted from Florence
Lost initials Oregon and
Who stole my heart
Their looks can you bear…
    Watching waves soar left
      As your arm is just right
DO THEY KNOW YOUR BEAUTY?
    Know your love
Think you are of it
I'd Never Dream Of
A face so precise
Regardless of light
I saw you shine in the red
Blossom with white
I tried to keep you
Keep you
Tight

You so blind

You so blind
You got bars
Banned from my strength
So you say,
It isn't so bad
You probably asked for it
Then you go off
Like before. Have you heard reality?
Abandoned for dead
When it's near
you so far

You so blind. You got bars
You think this so funny
You think you know
And I laugh back
Silently though
Because I may want to cry
And I know you're clueless
All I have left
Is pity
Or admiration
Because the only thing that sets
Our understanding apart
Is experience

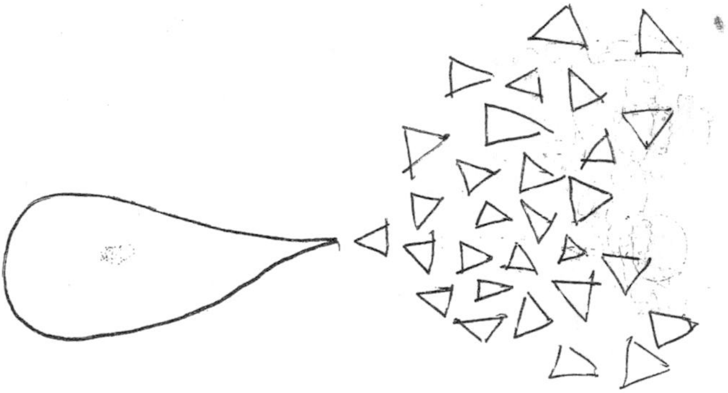

The Victim

He snatched me from sweet dreams
Into his nightmare
Every realm of existence I seek gone.
No recollection of anything satisfying anything happy.

My every breath every movement
Screams to take back the night. To be mine again.
As when the weary head tapped the soaking pillow.

Abused. Declothed. Hit. Smothered. Choked. Condemned.
Disrespected.
Over the night
Through the rising sun
Nature's beauty battling the ugliest sight imaginable.

That room. That morning.

Raped. Beaten. Tormented. Scarred.
Ripped of dignity. Vanished from existence.
Hopeless. Alone.
And trapped with the death of life.
Beauty of the Beast. In its most repulsive form.

Survival brings a new world.
One of simplicity. Childlike once again:
Because it is damned upon me.
I can forsee nothing.
What once was answered is back in questions.

Shocks. Scars.
The mirror is no longer my friend.
His ugliness is now mine too.
What's worse? Seeing myself?
Or allowing others to see me?

Words abruptly echo…memories. Continuously.
At unknown times.
His shadow continues down a body,
Once mine; but now questionable.
Bruises. Pain. Realism.

Hatred. I hate you.
Get off my face.
Get out of my mind.
Get away from my body.

Vanish. I do not want to be the victim.
I do not want the beast.
You are not for me.
You are not for me.

Sincerely,
Yours

Set Yourself Apart

I think the time has come for a revolution.
Together we find a way,
We know where we're going
When People aren't pushing us down
Telling us where to go
Round and round

Individualism conquers that percent.
It's not enough for what I'm talking about
Yeah,
A revolution
Revolt against the order
A pack of winners
Who'll change things around

Make us feel free again
It's been awhile
Since something like this happened

It's about time
We feel peace inside

Stay confident,
People of the revolution.
We are meant to rise
Not sink

Never Come Hither

Do you wish I do not heal? To wither
A way
Like a rotten-fair deal?
Is no mercy to be found?
I look the clown.
For in this race, I am walking.

Speed makes me empty
A rush
To rebound all the hate in my sight

You've found
There is no remorse
For you of course
Hitting the flat keys

Tuned in off key
As I wither
You never come hither

Loss of a loved one

When the Earth goes still
All is dim
I won't be in pain
I'll be thinking of him

I miss him so much
He had to go
He's the rain falling
The wind's echoes

I think I'm alone
The light blares
Can't see him or hear him
In my heart. Right there.

I take care of myself

I question your Faith.
I take my fate

I ponder your truth.
I play my tune.

I pet the snake.
I dress the slate.

I feel you in me.
I fall asleep.

I know I'm not dreaming for I feel the pain. The misery you've left me with is all I can claim. And all I can hope is that you I will see. I'm not making promises every day and it ain't many times that I claim to have a way.

What's left for all to do here? I don't see much. I can't continue this run around that's made me a mess. I wish for your solemnness. I wish for your grace. I wish that I'm not a disappointment in this race.

But I've done all I can in a world I don't understand. So here is the time I let go to let live. My agony has replicated to the point where I can not give anything more and mothering less. I'm not a heart breaker, I'm a soul maker. I'm not this persona but I'll live it my best.

Wake up sleepy head. Arise from the blunders. Please walk with me deep down under. Capture my realm. Captivate my presence. For it's the youthful at heart that don't belong in the thunders.

I'm not making memories I'm wasting time. Right now we need to fall forward, and combine. Making things happen is why I'm made for walking. Don't fall back, sweep gently onto my lap. Don't go. Don't go. But show yourself so I know.

Worthlessness

Mr. Trash, what are you doing here?
Forget wrong place at the wrong time.
You are the wrong thing.
The epitome of scum. The centre of cheapness.
Now showing...(drum roll please)...the Beauty of Karma.

You wouldn't know. Beauty is definitely not your think.
Hell is beautiful compared to you.
Spiders, bats, bees, roaches. All beautiful compared to you.
And I do think Marilyn Manson is beautiful.
You go with death maybe. But even death has some indirect beauty.

One thing you *may* be worth (unfortunately though since I really think you're worth nothing) is your own category to play in: SCUM
Yes you're cheap also but ugly cheap.
EVEN cheapness can be good sometimes.
DIE. SCUM. DIE.
Don't kill yourself; that would be too easy.
Your death can be purposely or by accident but definitely needs mass amounts of pain.
First, Ilena Bobbitt must rid you of your only friend given to you by accident when someone that you were worth it. HA!! What a joke.

While running, may you trip and may the insides of your misdirected head explode everywhere to only be washed away by the rain.

May you get paper cuts in a single file line, be victimized by a hive of bees and only hear the screeching of bats everyday until Jeffrey Dahmer comes for you and ultimately realizes you can't even be eaten.

I would've jumped on Helter Skelter before I choose you. At least he wasn't a coward and gets points for his efforts.

Even Satan himself won't let you in hell because you need to be worthy of it and we went through this before, you are worthy of nothing.

I

Definitely

Still

Don't want you.

It's a shame I've had to think of you this long.

May you be whacked with porcupine needles and have them nailed in.

That ought to show you the meaning of something.

It's called pain. Can you feel it, baby?

Then we need to burn those nasty wounds shut by rotating you over a burning roaster as you scream and cry for help while I make S'mores (event though I'm vegan but hey this is a special occasion).

Finally, I have some long overdue target practice I've been saving for my special someone starting with the good ol' bow and arrow right onto my rusty shotgun.

That should do you.

You're dead.

Bye. Bye.

January. February. March. May. April.
bring June. December. fades into
August. July.
come.
colder
when
September

Drop.

Drink. Decoy. Drops.
of. Dying. Months.

years. Days. Weeks.
MONTHS.

Tackle me. They Do.

They Tackle Me.
They Torture Me.
They Kill Me.

FINDING LOVE

Playground

Is love simply a playground?
      Playing around
        Toying with sounds
That are emotions.
Or is love a gas tank?
That always ends empty.

LOVE
Is a valley of trees
Fair leaves paired with their trees
Others down on their dead knees
Where they get thrown around.

I've heard love is two balloons
That go higher and higher
Until they fade and are drier
Even heard love is like an everlasting flame.
      A steady wind.
But I'm sure love
Is simply a playground

Pretty Boy

Pretty pretty boys – make for –pretty pretty toys
Pretty legs Pretty behinds pretty smiles
And every inch of you I adore. You're so pretty,
Pretty boy.

Oh boy, must I confess
I'm much too old for you
Your bed is much too small,
Find someone your own age to grow with
I've had those years now I'm full of knowin
You can' commit – the way I want to,
Little stud, grow up.

I'll paint a pretty picture of the disaster we would be
If I caved to your demands and became an ornament of your
love.

Succulent kisses make me smile
But petty grievances I have grown out of

I'm ready to give. You're willing to take
What sounds like a match could easily break

I'm burning up for your love but I've got to give it up
Love is a living thing. Our different ages beset different values.
I could be a disaster for you of loss, enabling, or destructive
separation.

You can not pull me down into old ways and sad days
For I'm letting go now. This is my goodbye
A gift to guide, my words will define what love can subside
Your pretty face will be my guide. I can not cry
This pretty thing has fallen
There's the door
I won't know no pretty no more.

Love Your Life

Paint me with your pain
And as the morning rises
I lie black as the abyss
Freckled with kisses
That killed my character
Crooked deeds
Cheap seats
Sneaky styles
Smart girl
When I walk away

You don't love me you love your damn self
U don't luv me u luv ur damn self
U don't luv me u luv ur damn self
U don't luv me u luv ur damn self
U don't luv me u luv ur damn self
U don't luv me u luv ur damn self
U don't luv me u luv ur damn self
U don't luv me u luv ur damn self
U don't luv me u luv ur damn self
U don't luv me u luv ur damn self
U don't luv me u luv my money

You hurt others until the only person left to hurt is yourself
You can even love yourself

Feelings

I was in a good mood.
All happy and gay
When I called him up,
I had so much to say

When he mentioned her,
It felt like a shot
Stung like a bee
And made me quite mad

Feelings are a lot,
Without them,
You're dead.
Just like the sun
When it's lighted red.

They mean a lot
Actually a tremendous, great deal
You can not lie
Not about how you feel

You're good for me

You knock just right
You're good for me, alright?
My start to the finish
I'll be there in your eyes
My ache goes away
I see what I have
It's you that comes to me
Allowances have given good grace
The songs you keep on
Integrity's not gone
My words retain honesty,
Honestly, perception you'll need
With no need and hesitation
This is not sounding a need for negotiations
I don't feel bad about any of it.

You're so very good for me & I thought you should know
You introduced yourself first. You allow me space.
You play songs for me. It frees me.
You knock just right. A manly man
Stong enough to stand alone
But no solitudes gold
Say "Dear, Bring your spirit a rest"
Gentle, this tough in your dome
Man, please bless at 10 o'clock
Dark and the moon gives off a spark
Die down with eyes so under

Weakness makes me grow
Let your sleep drum
All the way to morning
Spirit of yours way with mine.
I lay with time you are so good to me

Except you drink and you smoke
I barely even know you
Wouldn't know if it was true
For you
For me it was true
For you
For me it was twice
I don't want to rush this
Feeling stealing time away
I keep to contain in my memory like arms
As all I can say is you're good for me
If it don't last
If I don't match
I'll feel my way and I'll know
Existence is long
And I don't need to search
I found in you all I could void.

So very good you are
Very good for me
You are-so very-good, this good.
For me I'll tell you so.
Still leave and you will know.
So very good for me.

When we hold a kiss, it's more than a wish
That I will be good for you
If there's love it's like this

Reach or pray – this is it
Will be good-
If there's love it's like this
I, too, want to be so good for you

Lightbulbs

Your eyes taste of chocolate
Sweeter than sound sweeps
Across the ballroom floor. I see a delicate feather
Falling from the sky
When I look into your eyes
Safety, sorrow, simplicity, amorous
Despair of mine meeting the security
Eyes so dark turned, lighted
Marked green
Glowing with life
Gets me every night

Your crystal balls
A river of bliss, eyes of shells
Where I'm safe as pearls
They've got me. Captured.
Can you feel my soul
Swimming in your sea?
As they sparkle and shine
Staying secure
Invisible to love

The comforting tongue
Of your eyes alone
No disguise I'm at home
I'd die for your eyes
I'd live with that guide

Eyes can feel
When the body is still
I'm looking at eyes
Flowing high tides,
Your eyes

Passionate Times

Gently I come
Into the light of passion
It is not heat
Because heat exists in the heart
But when the heart is frozen,
Passion comes with light.
I carry that passion, burning bright

Although the hearth may vivaciously spill out in spurts,

It soon leaves,
Just like everything else must,
Goodbye heat of passion.
It was nice while it lasted
But now you too much go.

Just leave.
That makes it so much easier for me.
Please crush what has developed,
So I may be alone once again.
Tantalize my feelings some more if you must.
Leave me a colder heart than before.

Break my heart
Like I've broken so many before

The light of passion splashing and hashing
Until I feel so hot
Not heat. That's in the heart
When the hearts frozen
Passion is light
I'll carry that passion
Burning 'cause it's bright

Love lessons

Mountaintop.
Passing cloud.
Bicyclist.
Reveling.
Basking.
Giving.
Recurring.
Love.

Naming a house, hallelujah.
Praying with others.
Leadership-
Amongst criticism,
Complaints.
Finding your way through a maze.
It's all love.

When two people find each other,
And decide to spend their life together-
And do.
That's love.

Love is in me.
It's in you.
Let it out
In everything you do.

I'm loving time.
God teaches to.
He is love.
We all have it.

Abide to love
And, it,
Will abide to you.

Soul for a Dollar

I let me love. Did you love me?
Turn travesty into the taste of your lips
Again, it was more than a spurt of company.
Hours were against us – month passed by.
No space.
I want more. I am so selfish.
A fool. By vague and destructible tags.
There is not more to offer. I played well.
Sacred years of remaining spaces.

As it is – out in the cold, true love is sold.
Peasants pawned it for dollar; gave it up for freedom.
Didn't borrow, but it was used and destroyed, bought and
demolished.
I am annoyed.
Now that love has gone.
No space.
The days are aloof. Only society stands.
The pieces spread this.
For love blew over.
Back to a place it can never go again.

What?

Stars shine bright when
You are near.
Deep inside I clasp
A fear.
Will it all
Work out?
I think
So there is a doubt,
I want
To trust your words
But they fly away
With birds.

This thing feels hot.
I love
You a lot.
I hide
My frights
Though
Bright. Wide-eyed
Nights show
Pain
Remains
Inside. I run my
Self insane.

My love is blind.
I am me.
I am kind.
You're tearing me apart.
What
Are you
Doing to my heart?

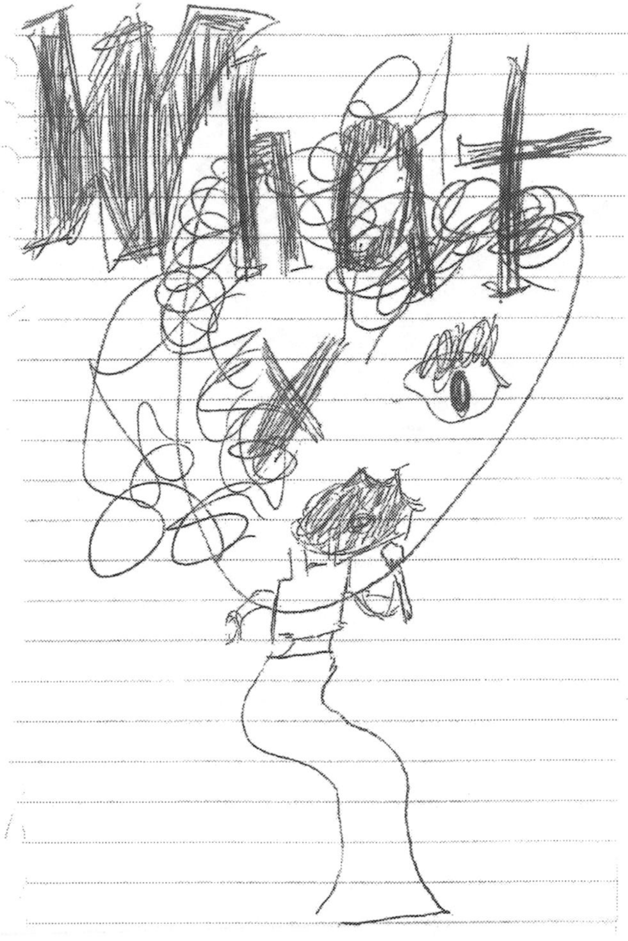
What

I WANT LOVE

This is my life and I'm giving it to you. Pride hate lust greed sloth envy…I'll keep love.

My love runs strong like the violator's wrong. 6 pence are hence thus the ones who become wise. I wander and I wander when will the jokes be done or could I possibly catch some truth in this maze I find running a loop in my head. A wandering wonder will take you deep down under and in here, as I'm reaching for the sun. I've been blue but I did keep my love and when I'm high like the sky will you be there like I am always true? Why oh why is the question with the most. Yet bringing it up makes everyone want to choke. Sitting. Searching. Reaching to a high that can be sustained. Lost boys and found friends stolen for nothing less than what I had hoped for. No, that's not the dope door. Cool as an eagle, my man must come singing songs of joy that may seem quite coy and what I am saying is how I got raying a bright light that's find and oh so right. Why I am under must be for your thunder. I want love.

Everyone will win and we all have to lose but all I can hope for is that sometimes I can choose what to keep true in my soul. It's strong. And it's pounding all night long. Every rainbow has different hues. Stick to your own kind and you'll only by singing the blues. Diversity happens to be the best key and that is the bridge to understanding me. You're swallowing wrong and you don't last very long. Please take the time to come by my side. Here you will see all things not wrong because what you get here is a refreshing son. What's all this huff about a weaker sex untough? Last becomes first in the race of the Earth. But it shouldn't be a controversy. What I just may have to do is huff and puff and blow you down. Dance I said.

Silence and solitude is not very hard to do. Finding a connection is not really something until you can conquer the small things and still be one with yourself. Little elves are really your friends in the grand race of time. In Life, you'll find them as your line. Follow the leader and take me deeper into grounds of affection and rhymes with perfection.

Moving too fast

I need you to be my friend – forever
You are my miracle
You are a bulb-you swore burned up long ago but just hadn't
been made use of
With me your feelings all come out
Part of why I'm with you has an answer flowing like a melody
taking out time with bass ball treble knees
You go up and you go down but you never go. Skip the scenario.
These old lives aren't where my flow in life goes.
I can never know what it would mean to honor a King.

Breaths of waves sweet whisper and a tongue with flares of red
in misty mornings when you're dreary it means everything,
That from this sullen face
You can shine solid of in arabesque

So blessed my state I shrug and wait for you to come thru the
door and what's important is not there no more

I call your name but it seems like a dream
If only to wake up was to see
That this state of bliss
My happiness, your sword was swiped from my care

Like a brick house
Each layer of brick makes it stronger

I know love. She lives with me. Don't ever leave me, love. Help me survive.

No boundaries/disrespect for when we love we are one with another.

I need you to be my friend.
Forever love me loving this.
When you're upset don't come at me
When you're happy think of me
When you're mad, I need love
These old lives aren't where were at the controversy can't be complacent.

I need you to look me in my eyes every single day when I'm away. Know I'm still fazed in them.

I need when you are weak to let me be strong.

I am so. Treat me fair. Get right up in there.

I need you to feel bad if you put it on me.
I need you to see it through if I confess to a mistake.
I need you to understand that when you really love me feelings like this never hurt anymore.

I want you always by my side. I could cry every time you're away. I sulk when you leave. I hope you know how much I appreciate it. It's a challenge for me to show.

I've felt this way once and I don't really want to again. How blessed I am to have you in my life. The only thing that rhymes is wife. I might have found all I need. You light my eyes my soul is free. The more we're together the less I'm away. Leave me now if you're back the next day. Your hair guides me down. My lips hear your sound. My ears need to know. Come together with you. It means I can. Jill, my dear. Be near.

Our words will say enough that we have two full lives left inside and every dream to finish aside.

Heart Against Mind

Flowing down the past
All the pricks I
'Bout what we had

Were you my lover?
Could I amount to just another?
Was I better?
Or Bitter

Why must I think?
I am fooling myself.
A fool to shelf.
"Put him away with the other."

"Letting go," sounds so easy.
Running should please me
But I go
Nowhere
Without my heart
And you've had it from the start

Let's get lost in a moment,
Stay together when groanin',
Caress my soft skin
Until my ego is thin,
In intimacy, time,
Mystery, wine,

I will always remember.

My heart says, "he's far
From a crook.
My mind, "don't even look."

Both are divine.
Too bad
We don't rhyme

When Love Lasts

When Love Lasts

Love is unending today
It leads with respect
On paths that make it turn and twist
Never waiting by the phone
You can see it's here to stay

Love lasts like valiant class acts
See rotating wheels and trims
That continue when we don't
Love resides inside of youth's
Fountain and living legends

Lasting love's in it falling
No waiting to ask. Observe
Forgiveness don't recall acts
It is in my tough skin, the bang
Of a pistol waiting guard

Where love lasts, adagio
Sunsets sparkle the landscape
Crystalizing my armor
Under a bright star falling
Touch makes way to caressing

Lasting love's worth money
Rare as one fresh red rose
Defined as a pink diamond

Pure as white satin. Centered
In my body like my ribs

When love lasts, a brush
Of the arm, a touch on the
Skin takes me to another
Level lacking remorse, pride
All, for the bold name of love

A candle burns where love lasts
Gentle nights, a light kill where
Betrayal holds no substance.
In the throes of mad passion,
Vanity is without face.

When love lasts the Earth stands still
A random touch takes a night
It lasts like the moon at night
Lasts and lasts like time though it's ticking
Love allows the boundless space

If love lasts I'll save my soul
Strong anchors on the sea,
Purple hearts ready to fight
The clear blue waters are in
Love's endurance and folly

Love lasts like the memory
Of two hands holding
A balloon shooting higher and
Higher and still higher
It does last. It really does.

Love lasts in the quiet winds
On a heat swelled, summer day
Pages of a bible
Brilliant minds brought together
You see the love I speak of

Sweet heaven when love lasts
Consistent spins on a fan
A jump rope slicing through the air
Lasts and lasts. It's really lasting
When love lasts. Oh, when love lasts

Yield

Brace yourself now
For what may arise
Will take you by surprise
It will shock
Leave you dismayed
Tease your temper
Deny your best attributes

That man is a killer
He'll hound you like a ghost
He'll break up the toast
Ruin a party
Destroy your good graces
Mock your class
Give you different faces

For if you're with him enough
You'll become the same
Watch yourself now
While you're still sane
Scotch it up now
You're going down in flames

Yesterday

I keep hoping for yesterday.
Not the liquor. Not the drugs.
I miss your cheerfulness
I miss our talks
I love your smile.
I love your smirk.
All you can be is a big bad jerk

I keep wishing for yesterday.
Not the smokes. Not the fights.
I miss good times.
Having you there.
I love your yap.
I love you.
I wish for you to say the same too.

Too bad for her.
Too bad for dawn
It's really too bad
Yesterday's gone.

No more

I never got pissed
When I couldn't
Pop from the top

Never before wished to climax
It's certain
What I want

I don't want to lose him.
Don't see him all year
And don't care.
It's alright to love.

Spellin it out
I L-O-V-E him

The person you are
I write off what you ain't

What's bad on others
L-O-V-E on you

The first we connected
I need more time to spend
L-o-v-ing him.
Don't care to again.

I've never been in love before.
It scares me.
Makes me sad.
I didn't try.

I wish he l-o-v-ed me
But we don't
Need to connect my love
With anything more
Than a feeling.

Serenity

Somewhere between
A child and a woman
I raise my weary head
Walk in steady set
Gently take the moment
Let it go – refuse to hold

Maketh my pathway
Along the flurry fauna
Flora in my hair
Contacts hold my stare
Like it's to be
Eyes tear every hour

Hounds on my side
Sadness cannot arise
No matter how I try
How touch things get
This moment's sent as my gift

I will respect that
And I will respect this

The Real Thing

You live your life pathetically.
Shame spills from your lips with the syllables
As you beg the world for pity on a shrunken soul.

Me.
I was a fool for falling in your trap only to be used
But the important thing
Is I'm not anymore
I know a broken record cannot be fixed.

It's worthless
As you, loverboy.
You are almost certainly repugnant
And do not realize how defying your every move is

So please step aside
I must soothe this soul
Brighten this life
Take the dreams home

Smoothly
Like Badu's strong songs
Fiona's jam in your face
I go now and pound on the piano
You are a waste of my time.
Even for pounding

My life still mine
My stars the city lights will keep shining
My music will float through the empty halls on a windy night
Over the houses
Under the heavens
My steering wheel virgin
My tongue stained
For never again will I allow another to do the same

You?
You are blessed with the memories
My grace to dream of
My subtle touch
My powerful movements
My strong head
I promise you can say goodbye to the real thing.

Connection

I see
You
Eyes
In me
Looking
At me
In me
I'm found within
Me
Trust what u see
Me
Here
Elevating my universe
Life lightened with you in it

Eager

A villanelle

He cannot approach the puzzle fast enough
Where she walks in a sullen state from a regretted room
And he steps to the point where their eyes can meet

The past fades away to the present time and day
Where he kisses her cheek and holds her hand.
He could not approach the puzzle fast enough.

She cuts for the feel. She skips her meal.
His dream at night is her to-be-wife.
He's ready to step to the point where their eyes can meet.

He's going to get down on one knee.
It is what he wants. Not sure what he sees,
And he cannot approach the puzzle fast enough.

They meet again or else it is loneliness.
She is clouded by thoughts that undress happiness
But he steps to the point where their eyes can meet.

All he wants is all she doesn't
He never asks but stays eager for lovin'
He cannot approach the puzzle fast enough
And he steps to the point where their eyes can meet.

Let me down

Love, let me down
Someone let me up for air – I plea
But he's gone
He just disappeared
I tear up
But he refused to catch them.
Did he when we were together?
Oh- how could a fool like me,
Be known to be so incomplete.
The love I have is real.
I know it is-
Maybe I'm not explaining it right
And my love will never come up.
So I'm drowning now
No man. No air. No excuses.
Why this constant reminder
That I am not enough?
I'm through with love.
Then I am. So, now,
I got it. Love

Layers of love

Layers of love
That never get touched
Yet still get up-
With a shoot it's a miss
On a kiss a mistake
It's like living without freckles
Crutches when you can walk
Checking in when you should leave
Those stinky shoes, no one knows
When black goes with white
Losing the ball for your hit
A shot on a foul
A gun when you're a vegetable
Life when it's been lived

Layers of love
Where a soul
Runs, shimmies, shakes, it erupts
To care for strangers
Wish for the endangered
It sets feed in the manger- what's stranger
It's like you
When you look at me like that

Still your weakness brings reticence
Expect me
To do it all
And I don't want to
But I have no choice
Feelings hurricane
My lips spread
Larynx loosens
Layers of love
That keep coming up

They are always falling down.
You see the spiral- now I mean
Much more

New Lovin'

If only you pleased me
I could be better
You wouldn't be changing my path
Getting your laughs
I provide
I give you what you need inside
But enough's enough
I haven't gotten pleased in a month

If only you pleased me
I could attach
Get emotionally wrapped and dramatic and attack
You with desires you can't give up
It'd be so easy
Really if you'd please me
And give your good lovin' up

If only you pleased me
I could get comfortable
Feel you are there
Tackle the big issues
Like what should I give you
But you haven't pleased me
I haven't been sleazy
So please me
It could be so easy

The last time:

This is it!

The last time he will hug at me
Be irritable. Have to do things his way.
This is the last blow up!

Yet, I give a little more.
I change.
Adjust to these scenarios.
I'm hardly evolving.

The animosity is maddening,
My calmness defying,
I feel a slow burn continuing
From our time together.
We've lost our temper enough,
And I need my sanity-
To retain what is mine.
Alone is where I may find
It to appear
From the darkness-clear;
No fog near.
This insanity has become comfortable
While your efforts have gone wild.
You've got some growing up to do.
This is my side.
Preserve. Protect. What I detect
Is too sad for words.

This love is dry.
I may cry
On my own time
For even I
Have become dislikeable
By people who like me.
I don't want to
Imagine the possibilities
Of staying with someone
Who cannot communicate,
Love or understand me,
Has nothing in it for me.
There are requirements of love, love,
Stipulations for someone to stay.
Love gives, receives and grows.
Oh, you don't know.
Respect hasn't grown.
So little you know.
You think I'm not good enough for you.
Well maybe that's true.

Merry Go Round

Love it. Hate. Desire all over my place.
Wait. I'll show you I care.
For you, my blood I'd bleed
Like my eyes do with you.
Look at my protracted pupils.
My oblong face sees
What you left as a legacy.
A universe was left to roam this cover
Kept on file so complete.
Wander round like a lover, if you tell me I am touch.
All I can give when happiness buckles.
Pain comes up. Makes me numb.
I could give all away and never have you.
I don't have time – I've had enough.
What I have in, every second is rough
My long desire is bursting. You ain't with me
What can I do to help you find me?
I kiss my freedom soft and sweet
So tell me "come back" come back"
I paint tears from heartache and night times survived on little
white lies
Disguise your whys and dream of this love
Find me so close when you hold fast in I that you have always
been dreaming of
I know happiness won't take every win. It talks a lot more than
it'll every back up

Mushiness makes vulnerable adults numb
Dumb. To love you so quickly to think that I've won
Dumb like clouds hide the sun
I gotta feel quick or my experience says I'll be losing the chance
of even a glimpse
When pain subsides and fills you up

When I see u again, it's a whole new lifetime
But I will love you like every moment you were mine
Let me come true.
You're enough for me I want this hurt I tend to the pain
I find myself causing violently causing each bad day
I wouldn't have that if we waited
If I knew you better
When you say you won't hurt me
Can you be a man stuck on your word
Now I'm worried
You'll say quietly it was in your eyes there
You want to be free, can't keep my house key
If you don't want to see me ever again
Fine with me
Anything you want, my friend

Love or something like it

Is it one night
Or is your speech eternal
Id like you to see what's in store
Is there more?
Let that light burn in your brain
Flood it in grail
It's just your eyes pressing me
Do I come out all right?
A dark urge has you talking romance
My red lips are numb
Pull me over. Slow me down.
Two can become one.
So shiny you should swipe me
I adore-now I'm asking for more
Do you wanna hear this?
I adore. Share this talk.
You've been fun.
Let's pin it down to tonight
One night.
Definitely not love.
You said I didn't axe the talk
Thrill of spittin peeps
Froth isn't real

Is it love?
Seems just one night
Speak eternal
Of listening
You'll see when in embrace now
Come to not disrupt
Consider it too wants love
This moment is eternity
So let it be
Or let me relive
The hustle hassle society
Is gone tonight
Like Pez pills your generosity offered me
I've got sincere varieties torn info
Runs of veins shedding skin rough
Around the edge
Where do I stand
Living around every clock has it's place
I didn't see desperation there, man

Living apart

Every day, I walk the way to your door.
The bridge seems to take forever some days.
"Keep up separated, "you said, so we live apart.
I know, too, that it's better this way.
We aren't living together even if our lives encourage it.

I walk this way everyday and you expect this from me.
On my way to your door today I felt a bit funny.
When my foot touched the floor in the morning
I was feeling quite fine- like a supersonic force
But as the day drift on I lost my thunder.

You got me feeling alright, but ashes have no place.
All that's left are remains.
In esthetics, you could grow. With grace, you should know
Love is not potential. It exists. It just is.
You're not here. You're always at home.

I have a long walk to where love exists.
It should be inside it should be here
That's what love is, and with you I no longer see it
You want to keep us separated and now we will be.
I'm getting weaker so you're leaving gracefully,
Here's my send off. I know when I reached the bridge.

Buck them

If I could call you that word
It'd never come out still
Id be stuck
Surrounding the space like I'm the circumference
All around my fate. Word that echoes
When it haunts it makes no woman soft.
Looking at your scar
Trying to act hard
And trying to find out where you were going
Forgives this couple on its lost
Cause I wanna go
I saw you get your coat on
And there's people, you can buck them, without me.

Loving

I'm here. Now. I'm living.
I'm life. I'm love. I'm here for a reason
That's what keeps me going.
There haven't been any accidents in my past.
Everything I've been through offers me something.
Something to give. Something to learn from. Something to gain.
I'm loving right now.
This is love.

Codependent

I am a radical woman.
I want what you want.
So, let me help
So we can set it right.

Examples Needed

How big is wonderful?
Is love that? Or is it mundane,
A small thing, a little glitch?
If it grows I know-
It must be great.
I hate to complicate.
These things I contemplate.
Being alone
My love has no home.

A beautiful thing-what is it?
Does it feel good all of the time?
Can I calculate it? Rewind?
Stop! This is absurd.
It can't be that hard
What if I am- simply
Not the settling kind!

Are there requirements of love?
Does it just show up?
Answer me, please.
I need to know!
Soon I will have no family left
And it will be a small funeral at my death.

I don't mean to be trite.
I have no insight of which can provide light.
My days are looking gloomy.
Without a love, I live rudely.

So, let me practice love.
Enjoy my life.
Bring in light.
I'll learn what I'm missing.
Stop all the dissing
And get to kissing.

Love can't be that hard.
May be that's just me.
Will I find it if I look?
Is it coming soon?
Will it reside?
Tell me
Or just forget it.

False bravado in the name of Love

Love
I am grateful for love
Companionship, reciprocity, integrity
Social intelligence, manners
Acts of kindness
Gestures of affections

How, my baby,
Can you find a way to say you have love for me-
When you do none of the above?
Let's not pretend.
I know what it feels like to love-and to be loved.
Nothing of the kind when we're alone or out or anywhere for
that matter.

This matters to me.
I was told, follow your bliss.
What then keeps me to you?
There is nothing to attach to
It's like we don't belong
Here
My gratitude speaks for this ending
My time will be filled with love
I can recognize I give in to
That respects me
Of which is that page I fall on
You're stranger
And right now, I'm grateful for that

Walk Away

When I don't tip,
Make a rude remark,
Saying the wrong things,
Writing the wrong words,
Living the wrong way,
And playing rap songs

When I don't sleep
And interrupt your privacy-
I'm telling you to listen.
This is serious.

When I'm away a lot
And telling lies.
When I say your poem sucks,
When I act like a fool

When I don't pay for anything,
When I don't listen.
When I don't get you nothing for Easter
Or Christmas.
I'll remember your birthday
But make sure you tell me that day.

When I'm snoring in that cute way,
When I'm paying attention to someone
Beside you
Then you need to walk away

Smooth Hustla

Description:
A lady. A "man."
No shaky hands
Or uninvolved stands.

There's passion
But it's what you miss.

Clothes gotta come off
With heat
For you to see it.

All the working on the ground.
The ease,
The fruit,
The juice,
She grows.

Just a smile
Not a mess
Of attitude
Cause this groom's good

Getting good
And better
But it'd never set off the alarm,

It's clean lining.
Operating like a fireman.

Is that how you'd walk in?
All calm.
Right before the burn sweeps your face

Ah, no,
Cause disaster's very rare to come.

Such a small percentage
If you live
Through it
You'll make up for all the people
Who'll never get in.

It takes so strong long-
To get over-
Just keep getting it-
Long after it's gone.

Forget how memories work.
Forget what happens.
Life knows.
Just keeping it hustla.
One night you went under.

Curl up! Swirl out…
Til you cold as an ice cream cone.
No feeling there.
Let 'em back
But they're gone.

Smooth hustla
Keep on hustling
That love will find you
When you're ready

When You Go

I called today.
You were away.
The message said
I'd call back again.

This isn't very easy.
The song's here to free me.
I must go on and
What I remember of you
Is going to make me strong

When you go
Please remember
I'm back here
Thinking of you

One

You,
You were the one
The one I found
Apart from the others

You played a new groove
This I won't lose

You were the one
Burning fires instead of graves
You were here to stay
Captured by your flame
I did not see
I would melt away

Can you feel the heat?
Taking you over
Burning me under
Clouding like thunder

You were the one
Quarrels became chaos
You took everything in sight
I never knew
I wasn't up for the fight

You were the one
You hid all my scars
You brought me back again
Under now
Letting you go
We'll be one again

Lover Lover

You told me not to whisper.
Those whispers
Are the only peace I know.

You told me my life is a game.
The only one
You kept me from winning

You told me, please,
Learn to wait
For what's new
Will become old

Yet still I knew
That I shouldn't have to

Lover, lover
Why?

You tell me.
I ask questions.
Why?

Ahh That We Are

Late at night
I dream of you
Thinking about
What we could do

I want to hold you
Dance the night away

All day long
I'll walk the streets
Yearning for us
To meet again

Ahh dream of you
Ahh love you
Everything's so meant to be
We go together
Like 1, 2, 3

In my head
You're the one
For me
All I say
It's plain to see
Where I wonder
Will be with you
Reaching out

For where we met
What I meant
Is what I said
I just can't
Get you out my head

Ahh dream of you
Ahh love you
Everything's so meant to be
We go together
Like 1, 2, 3

A perfect match
In a world
A mess
Nothing more
Nothing less
Let's allow
Our bodies to become one
A perfect match
We will be blessed
All this time
I've found much less
Let's allow
Our bodies to come one cause

Aah dream of you
Aah love you

Aah dream of you
Aah love you

LOVE

Love

Only

Verifies

Everything

LOVE

Letting me

Open up to

Verify

Everything about you

The

End

MEOW

About The Author

Jill Niebuhr is an award winning poet. She has been featured in shows and highlighted as a favorite by attendees. She has always written, receiving recognition and advancement for her writing.

Ms. Niebuhr is also known as artist Jmn ("jammin"). She penned a hip hop album, Fresh Blood. She plays piano, makes beats, and sings. She has played in a band and will continue her work as a musician.

She is getting a degree in politics now. This allows her to think creatively about solutions and use her public speaking ability to inspire others.

After suffering much tragedy and moving around a lot, she now lives as a single Christian in Saint Peter, Minnesota.

Printed in the United States
By Bookmasters